Guiding Motivations:

Messages through Trials, Tribulations,

and Tests

Prince F. Robertson, M.S. Ed.

ISBN-10:1978424698
ISBN-13: 978-1978424692

This book is lovingly dedicated to my children:

Jeremiah Prince Robertson
Isaiah Fredrick Robertson
Danielle Barbara Robertson

I pray this body of work leaves a blessed and lasting legacy.

GUIDING MOTIVATIONS

TABLE OF CONTENTS

ACKNOWLEDGMENTS

The Almighty Father has spiritually guided this book, but I would like to thank those who have assisted me with bringing my vision to light through publication and visualization. Dr. Eugene Moore, Darryl Cowans, Vernique Jackson of Vee Jay Nicole Consulting Group, Thomas Settle of BigVisions, Dr. Tyra Seldon of Seldon Writing Group, and my loving wife Mallory N. Robertson.

All of those who have guided me spiritually and mentally throughout my journey and those whose shoulders I stand upon.

Spiritual Guidance: Reverend Charlie B. Cross, Reverend Karen Cross, Reverend Reginald Johnson, Reverend Larry D. Lewis, Reverend Flinnoia Hall III, Reverend Dr. Desmon Daniel, Reverend Adrian Johnson, Reverend Willie Branch, and Reverend John Range.

Educators: Dr. Saran Donahoo, Dr. Emanuel Lalande, Casey Cornelius, Willie E. Thompson (Deceased), Crasha Townsend, Father Joseph Brown, Dr. Tasha Toy, Cletra Peters, Dr. Dwaun Warmack, Dr. Raphael Moffett, Dr. Dhanfu Elston, Reynolda Brown, Cynthia Polk-Johnson, Deneen Adams, Dr. Leonard Gadzekpo, and Dr. Deborah Barnette.

Community Leaders: Rhonda Butler, Lee Arthur, Jr., Julian Taylor, Sr., Saginaw Valley African American Leadership Training Institute (SVAALTI), First Ward Community Center, Patricia Avery, NAACP (Champaign County Branch), Delta College, and Kappa Alpha Psi Fraternity, Inc., - Saginaw Alumni Chapter.

Inspiring Confidants: Tamario Howze, Nathaniel Banks, Nate Randall, Mike Henderson, Ardayell Brewer, Kelli Bond, De'Niel Phipps, Robert Liddell, Shyvonda Pritchett, Jason C. Brown, Dave Chester, Dwarne McNair, Sr., Patrick Reynolds, Thomas Mathurin, and The Davis/Gilliam/Smothers Families.

Siblings: Nkrumah Grant, Pierre Grant, Courtisha Grant, Khadim Fall, Khoudia Fall, and Eustace Hawker.

Lastly, my mother Dolorese P. Grant-Fall with her infinite love & grace, Step-Father Moudou Fall, and the Grant family.

FOREWORD

I have had the distinct pleasure of knowing Mr. Prince Robertson for over a quarter of a century. We initially met during his educational endeavors when I served as a high school teacher and Mr. Robertson was a student. Although he was a phenomenal track and basketball athlete, many people thought that Prince would not graduate from high school. Against many naysayers' thoughts, Prince graduated and later became a collegiate student-athlete; he even played college basketball under my leadership. It didn't take long for me to notice his great potential; therefore, I have advised him in his academic, social, and professional endeavors. It's been an extreme pleasure to observe and be a part of Prince's growth as a God-fearing man, husband, father, son, brother, minister, and mentor.

Whether you are in Christian ministry or you have a desire to connect with mankind, I believe that this book is a must read for individuals of every age. Prince Robertson has the unique tasks of educating various age groups in the areas of both carnal and spiritual intelligence. He uses his God-given talent as well as his academic background to capture and teach the important communication and relationship skills that we all need in order to be successful. Throughout this book, Prince uses his diverse religious, educational, and cultural experiences and connects them to God's Holy scriptures. This not only makes his points more vivid, but it also helps readers make connections between the text and their lives. His ability to capture these rich life messages in writing speaks volumes about his level of spiritual awareness: past, present, and future.

Using God's holy and timeless scriptures, Prince looks to align today's language and social attractions with the unchanging word of God. Understanding that only the things that we do for God will last, this book's foundation is built on God's word. It is enlightening to see the work of a now colleague shed light for a dark generation. *Guiding Motivations: Messages through Trials, Tribulations, and Tests* will not only strengthen the Saints of God, but it will draw those who don't quite understand closer to the great creator. Through deep meditation and reflection upon this book, many souls will be saved and lives will be enriched—all to the Glory of GOD!

-Pastor Flinnoia Hall III

INTRODUCTION

I was born in New York City where the St. Nicholas Housing Projects in West Harlem was my home until the age of 13. I'd be lying if I said it was easy; my family and I had good days, but they were also plagued by a share of bad days. Nowadays, when I explain to friends and colleagues how Harlem was in the 1980-90s, I usually tell them they can believe a little more than half of what they've seen depicted on the television. Heading into my 8th grade year, my mother moved my siblings and I to Daniel Heights Housing Projects in Saginaw, MI. This is a place I immediately loved as my new home. I was befriended by many and bullied by some, yet all the experiences helped to build me into the man I am today.

As far as I can remember, I've always been different in my own right. At times, I believed that the cards were intentionally somehow stacked against me. But, as I let my life instances mold me, I recognized that it all was for good reason. I believe it was to give me a story, or stories to use as encouragement to continuously build resilience. Like others, it wasn't easy growing up without a father and it still isn't an easy pill to swallow today. I often think about how different my character and personality would have been if he were in my life.

It also wasn't easy being the kid always known to act out, to be verbally and physically disciplined due to being misunderstood because I lacked having a strong male authority. It wasn't easy being told by relatives that I have "no luck" or being written off by others as one with no solid future. I want you, as readers, to know that amid the many negatives of life, there is light, and there is nothing more motivating than to have one's future spoken upon and compared to alcoholics and failures. It's one of the best ways to stay encouraged and motivated.

God in his infinite wisdom saw fit to place me in the midst of everything I went through to create the strong husband, father, spiritual leader, mentor, role model, and educator that I am today. I've learned that where one individual may be indifferent about you, there may also be two who believe in you more than you believe in yourself. In this book, you will read 10 different, yet connected messages of trials, tribulations, and tests that I have endured, and am still enduring. These instances have groomed me spiritually to overcome several obstacles set in my path. Through biblical context, and constantly being connected to Christ, I found security, safety, and stability.

My hope is for you to read these messages and to receive the similar refuge that I have received throughout the years.

Let these messages guide and motivate you, and in the end, be a blessing to you!

-Prince F. Robertson, M.S. Ed.

I
DO IT FOR THE VINE

1 I am the true vine, and my Father is the gardener. 2 He cuts off every branch in me that bears no fruit, while every branch that does bear fruit he prunes so that it will be even more fruitful. 3 You are already clean because of the word I have spoken to you. 4 Remain in me, as I also remain in you. No branch can bear fruit by itself; it must remain in the vine. Neither can you bear fruit unless you remain in me.
John 15: 1-4 NIV

When reading this scripture, I automatically remembered a social media clip of a little girl who, in my opinion, popularized the phrase: "Do it for the vine" and the popular social media app *Vine*. When reading this message, I won't be referencing the viral video of children creating dance routines. However, I'll be explaining how the vine holds true to those who are Christ fearing in a different light. There is a deeper meaning in what the vine truly is, what it does, and what it can do for you as a believer. When we talk about the vine as it relates to scripture, we must understand the importance of it and why we should continuously make it a priority to be connected to it. My goal is to enlighten you, so when you head back out into the "world" from beyond your four walls, you will be able to reach out and touch others with the hope that they too will believe and be connected to the vine.

So, what is the vine? What happens when we are not connected to it? In this message, I'll present three topical points when answering the aforementioned questions—falling short of the vine, lifeline to the vine, and benefits of believing in the vine.

1 I am the true vine, and my Father is the gardener... *John 15:1 NIV*

The speaker in this text is Jesus Christ, and here he clearly tells us that he is the true vine. With knowing that, I can probably conclude this message, but, what would this guiding motivation be without testimony? I believe that with the support of the Holy Bible, we should all be connected to the vine. Why? Because we all fall short of the vine and of the glory of God, and by having a guide to refer to in times of despair or stress, it provides us with sweet words of comfort. If we all fall short then that means we are not perfect; this means that we will always be in need of spiritual help and forgiveness.

So, because we all fall short and are not perfect, we tend to act without compassion and love. We lash out verbally at others, we roll our eyes at people we don't like, we criticize, judge, and do much more. My students would usually coin these behaviors as "throwing shade". Unconsciously, most of these behaviors are committed through a strange and unwanted spirit. Understand that as believers, because we fall short, it doesn't necessarily mean we are not connected to the vine, but it doesn't make it alright either. Understand that being connected to this true vine will give us grace, mercy, and forgiveness if we possess it in our hearts.

I fell short a while back as I lashed out at one of my fraternity brothers. As a young minister in training, understand that I am not exempt. I too battle issues within as I walk through this world. I lashed out at him verbally in an authoritative manner which showed a lack of leadership. As he sent a text message to fellow members of the executive board, I overstepped my boundaries in demanding that he send specific communication to the fraternal body. I, in fact, was out of bounds in demanding that he communicates inaccurate information. This was an attempt to abuse my leadership as vice-president. This was also a moment of falling short as I verbally lashed out, unknowingly. I ultimately saw the error of my ways and apologized to him face to face, asked for his forgiveness, and reiterated how it was inappropriate for me to communicate with him in an unprofessional manner. I, then, let him know that we, who are called to deliver God's messages, often make mistakes as anyone else, even when we are connected to the vine.

2 He cuts off every branch in me that bears no fruit, while every branch that does bear fruit he prunes[a] so that it will be even more fruitful. 3 You are already clean because of the word I have spoken to you.
John 15:2-3 NIV

This vine is our lifeline to promise, favor, forgiveness, grace, and mercy. But most importantly, this vine is our lifeline to Christ. Believing in this vine wholeheartedly gives us restoration and reassurance. Believing in this vine gives us the desires of our hearts, but, we must remain connected to it.

We must remain in this vine and believe this same vine resides in us. Thinking of this vine as a lifeline to Christ prevents us from doubting. When we find ourselves at a hurdle that seems too high to get over, leaning on the belief of this lifeline to the vine should strengthen us and remove that doubt.

I once had a conversation with a good friend who is also in the ministry. He explained to me that his daughter had been battling a decision that would uproot her and her son to a different city and state across the country. His daughter had no financial plan, neither did she have a concrete plan for stable housing. The only motive that his daughter had was that she needed a new start. As I listened to my brother in Christ, the only thing I thought about was faith. I explained that we, as parents, have a natural tendency to worry about our children. But, I also explained to him that as ministers, we must do our best to practice what we preach by leaning on faith, praying about it, and trusting God. Being connected to the vine should instill that faith.

I then thought about my own battles as it relates to being connected to the lifeline within the vine and trusting God. I have an 11- year old son who has autism, and is considered to be "high functioning". We, as a family comprised of my wife and two sons, have been Illinois residents for over three years now. A fear of mine was uprooting him again to another state due to the ambiguity of my profession. We had already moved from Michigan to Illinois, Illinois to Florida, and back to Illinois again. I had a fear of moving him out of a great school system and risk placing him in a situation where a new school wouldn't be able to meet his special needs. I also thought about him making new friends and getting used to a new city and its surroundings. I worried about him growing up and lacking some sort of stability as it relates to being rooted in one area. Being connected to the vine afforded me to have a spiritual conversation with God to give me comfort in my decision-making process.

Instead of focusing on the negatives, I repositioned my train of thought to think positive. I focused on the faithfulness of the Lord, and what it meant to have unwavering faith. Professionally, I don't know where I will be in the next 3-5 years, but what I do know is that God has a plan and rewards all those who believe wholeheartedly in him as the vine. When faced mentally with odds, take time to pray about it and trust God, and in the end, you will be provided with an answer. Believe in the lifeline that is the true vine, Jesus Christ.

5 I am the vine; you are the branches. If you remain in me and I in you, you will bear much fruit; apart from me you can do nothing. 6 If you do not remain in me, you are like a branch that is thrown away and withers; such branches are picked up, thrown into the fire and burned. 7 If you remain in me and my words remain in you, ask whatever you wish, and it will be done for you. 8 This is to my Father's glory, that you bear much fruit, showing yourselves to be my disciples...
John 15:5-8 NIV

Believe in the vine, stay connected to the vine, just as the vine wants to be in you and you will receive much benefit and reward. If you believe, whole heartedly, and have patience, whatever you want, you will receive. But always remember to be realistic. Let's say that a desire of yours is to possess an abundant amount of money. Will your church see expansion through tithes and offering? Will an agency catered to helping others see a selfless donation? Will the community be watered with gifts to assist in bringing people to the church and to Christ? What I'm saying is if you don't find balance within your blessings, you will be humbled. The alternative may be God using you as a hard lesson as he slowly takes away that abundant amount of money for lack of humility.

9 As the Father has loved me, so have I loved you. Now remain in my love. 10 If you keep my commands, you will remain in my love, just as I have kept my Father's commands and remain in his love. 11 I have told you this so that my joy may be in you and that your joy may be complete. 12 My command is this: Love each other as I have loved you. 13 Greater love has no one than this: to lay down one's life for

one's friends. 14 You are my friends if you do what I command. 15 I no longer call you servants, because a servant does not know his master's business. Instead, I have called you friends, for everything that I learned from my Father I have made known to you. 16 You did not choose me, but I chose you and appointed you so that you might go and bear fruit—fruit that will last—and so that whatever you ask in my name the Father will give you. 17 This is my command: Love each other…
John 15:9-17 NIV

There are indeed benefits of staying connected to the vine. I went to high school with a couple of brothers and I knew that their parents were believers in the Lord. Their father was a principal and their mother worked in the medical field. These were the type of kids that you knew would be something special in the future. Their upbringing was held to a certain standard of knowing right from wrong, being compassionate, loving, and understanding. Not once did I see these brothers lose their cool, display disrespect, and they always seem to have great composure. They went on to college and both became doctors and are now making a major difference in their everyday lives. I personally believe that this was rooted in their parents being connected to the vine. Their parents then reaped the benefits by having two successful sons. The two brothers did what they were supposed to do within their own right, and are now, too, reaping the benefits through their success.

My journey was a bit different. Although I was connected to the vine at a young age, I faced a lot of trials and tribulations. Mostly, they were the result of not being as obedient as I should have been. I was the high school kid who gave moms and dads high-blood pressure and headaches. I didn't go to class; my grades suffered tremendously; and my grade point average was horrible. I would always get to a certain point in my defiance and jump, without any regards. However, I was also given grace and mercy. I believe

Christ, who gave himself for my thoughtless acts, always stepped in right on time. Through the divine intervention and me recognizing my inner gift of determination, I was able to defy the odds with resilience. I may not have graduated from high school on time, but, I eventually graduated. I may not have received my bachelor's degree in the traditional 4 years, but, I received that too, all while struggling to raise my son who was diagnosed with autism. I also was confronted by several challenging, yet life changing events that gave me the inner fuel needed to pursue my master's degree of education. All of this, I believe, were benefits of staying connected to the vine and recognizing who is my true rule and guide. I urge you to love each other, love on your neighbor, and know that Christ is your lifeline. Know that we all fall short, and know that we receive spiritual benefits, but remember to always remain connected to the vine.

II
FIX IT LORD, FIX IT

14 Your offspring shall be like the dust of the earth, and you shall spread abroad to the west and to the east and to the north and to the south, and in you and your offspring shall all the families of the earth be blessed.
Genesis 28:14 ESV

The one thing that taints our soul is the very entity that has taken most of our lives by storm—social media! Facebook, Instagram, Snapchat, and Twitter are some of the most popular platforms. All of these social media entities, if not deciphered or explained carefully, can ultimately divide, not only our youth, but families all together. It'll send confusion throughout the household, and we all should know by now that the devil is indeed the author of confusion. If we plan to have a lasting spiritual relationship with our spouse and have Christ in the midst of it, the very thing we cannot do is be influenced by the internet or social media. We sometimes find ourselves comparing our relationships and families to others that we have seen online, and this is something we must stay clear of, especially when there's a possibility that it may be fabricated. Every household and every relationship is completely different; it's like a puzzle piece, no one relationship is identical to another relationship. All we can do is be ourselves. Over a year ago, I spoke to my fellow church members about accepting, believing, and having faith in Christ. Here's a simple formula my wife and I use.

Hopefully, it will assist you in your own respective relationships while ultimately assisting you in developing your family. My hope is that this message equips you with the proper basics on how a man and woman, a husband and wife, or engaged couple, can not only build each other up, but construct a foundation to build or save their family. I want you to understand the importance of being virtuous, having spiritual strength, faith, and patience.

It's not easy to always work together, and sometimes we tend to fall apart as husbands and wives or as courting couples. But I implore you to do like my wife and I by simply and constantly asking the Lord to fix it. Let's start with the importance of the Virtuous Woman.

Ideally, it is God's plan for every woman to be virtuous. But a good and virtuous woman is hard to find, and worth far more than diamonds and rubies. Don't get me wrong, no one is perfect, but a virtuous woman is able to notice her own value, her vocation, and her strength. Think about a mother in the context of the upbringing of a child. Mothers are teachers; mothers are disciplinarians; mothers are cleaning ladies; and mothers are also nurses, doctors, psychologists, counselors, chauffeurs, coaches, and the roles go on and on. Mothers are developers of personalities, molders of vocabularies, and shapers of attitudes. Mothers are soft voices saying, not only to children, but to others… "I love you, baby". "You got this". "It's gonna be alright". Most importantly, mothers are a link to God; they are a child's first impression of God's love. In Proverbs 31, verse 23, the bible speaks of the virtuous woman's husband. It tells us that he is **known in the gates, when he sits among the elders of the land.** In the middle of a lengthy description of the woman, out of that entire scripture of Proverbs 31, it talks about her husband. A woman, working *together* with her husband,

14

can have tremendous impact on their success. I attended Southern Illinois University Carbondale during the years of 2011-2013. During this time, my family and I leaned on faith and gathered as much as we could take with us and headed to Southern Illinois to prepare a new life for ourselves. I was blessed to receive a graduate assistantship in University Housing/Residence Life through a lengthy interview process. My wife and I were already homeowners through an inherited house; we had two vehicles and both had jobs. I felt God communicate to me that it was time to move.

When you witness God's communication as a believer, it would behoove you to listen. My path was to go through a rigorous graduate program that has led me to now be employed at a top tier university in the nation, the University of Illinois at Urbana-Champaign. The transition wasn't easy and we had our days and nights of struggle. I am a true believer that God anointed us for this journey because it was only by his grace that we financially survived with roughly $600 a month for a 4-person household. In order to financially survive, we couldn't afford two car notes so we had to sell one of our cars. We then were forced to give our second vehicle back to the dealership. We also had to become recipients of public assistance again, receiving food stamps and Medicaid.

It was rough because we felt as if we had gone backwards—from homeowners, two cars and two incomes to one car that we could barely afford and living in a two-bedroom apartment in a residence hall. In the end, through all of the struggles, sacrifices, and hardships, we made it through. We did this not separately, but together as husband and wife by working together to generate tremendous impact for our future success.

Now the tables have turned; my wife has graduated with her graduate degree in Social Work (MSW) and the same support she afforded me was naturally returned. We are slightly better off financially; we both have a steady income, reliable vehicles, and a sufficient roof over our heads. During her journey while receiving her MSW, my wife took 20 credit hours, worked nights, and we've dealt with the passing of both of her parents. But look how God works, as a virtuous woman, her strength and faith continually shines through. Her hard work was recognized by her Social Work Program; she was presented with a financial award for hard work while maintaining her grades and enduring hardships through her program. I do my best to support her as we unify as a virtuous couple. Working together will, of course, be beneficial to the development of our union, but it is also to the benefit of our children. We are more concerned with their future and the ability to set great examples for our two sons and daughter.

I believe in all that we do, we should consider how it will affect our children and any child, youth, or teenager whom we have a strong influence upon. As I think about working together, a funny story comes to mind. My wife and I watched a comedian on television awhile back; he made a joke about how he and his wife "tap out" when they get too frustrated helping their son with his homework. Anyone who knows us Robertsons know how animated we are. We decided to take the same approach that this comedian used. As Jeremiah, our 11-year-old, was working on his homework, he had an issue comprehending a specific math problem. I'd been at work all day and I was short tempered and couldn't figure out why he wasn't grasping the mathematic problem. My wife noticed my frustration; she walked over to the kitchen table, touched me on my shoulder and said: "tap out baye". We then switched off on helping Jeremiah figure out one of his many math problems. But something happened; I saw that she started to get frustrated. I then walked over with a smirk on my face, touched her on the shoulder and told her "tap out sweetie". I then took over in pursuit of assisting our son with his homework. It wasn't ideal, but we worked through it; we worked together. We trusted each other all while leaning on the faith we already possessed knowing that we can get through anything together.

29 He gives strength to the weary and increases the power of the weak.
Isaiah 40:29 NIV

No man is perfect. You see, we, as men, have this friend called an ego, and attached to this friend is his buddy pride. And once these two friends get together, it becomes an opportunity for destruction. I know how ego and pride are because I speak from experience. We have this ego friend that speaks for us and makes irrational statements to his significant other like "I'll be back when I get back" if we were asked a simple question like where we're going and how long we'll be gone. That same friend ego will also speak for us by saying, "I run this house, not you" when asked something as minute as if a certain bill was paid. God gives strength to the weary, not the foolish. We then have that other friend who appears at times, pride! Pride will speak for us and say, "I ain't working at McDonald's! I'd rather stay right here and wait for someone else to call." Pride would even go as far as speaking for us and saying, "I don't want you getting a job, I'm the breadwinner." That's not the type of behavior that gets rewarded. Breadwinners don't sit at home and wait. Breadwinners get out and cut the grass with scissors if necessary to make financial ends meet and to put food on the table. When ego and pride pull you away from humility, it stunts your spiritual growth. Lack of spiritual growth in the family leads to dysfunction. A family in turmoil from the results of dysfunction taints our future. And that future is our youth. As men, we need to do away with ego and pride, especially if we are in a relationship with a virtuous woman. We owe her an explanation every time she asks where we're going and when we'll be back. That has nothing to do with being soft. If we don't have a job, or if we are struggling to find our way financially, all we can and should do is stay diligent and humble no matter how weary we may get and no matter how weak we may feel at times. If we have truly accepted Christ and have faith in Him, guess what? As stated in the scripture above, *29 He gives strength to the weary and increases the power of the weak.* Men, our ego shouldn't be too big to go to the Lord when we're in need and our pride can't be bold enough to not humble ourselves unto Him. All we have to do is have strength enough to say, "Fix it Lord, fix it", and with conviction and confidence, it will be.

We tend to compare our lives and relationships to those on Facebook and social media. I too am guilty of posting pictures of my wife and making statuses about our relationship, and of course telling funny stories about my two sons. We cannot get caught up in what everyone else is doing. It is very easy to get a distorted idea of the definition of a man and a woman these days, especially if we rely on social media. We must all realize that there is no such thing as perfection. You have the ability to be what God has intended for you to be. Did you know that there are two women of the Bible (Ruth and Ester) in which a book is named after? Of these two women, Ruth is the only woman in the Bible specifically said to be virtuous. I want you to know that what Ruth displayed is a great example of how to be virtuous in a corrupt world. Ruth teaches us that becoming a woman of noble and faithful character is attainable through God's grace. Ruth replied to her mother-in law in scripture saying,

16 Don't urge me to leave you or to turn back from you. Where you go I will go, and where you stay I will stay. Your people will be my people and your God my God. 17 Where you die I will die, and there I will be buried. May the LORD deal with me, be it ever so severely, if even death separates you and me.
Ruth 1:16-17 NIV

We're going to have some hardships and some rainy days. We're going to go through a time when all you can do is cry. But, if you can find the strength to get on your knees, as believers, and simply say, "Fix it Lord, fix it", I can guarantee that in God's time, all will be well.

I often get asked by younger couples how it feels to be married with children. And, of course, I would tell them it's a blessing. I also tell them it's not perfect. Think about it, if we, as the Lord's children, are not perfect then how can our marriages be? So, I tell them that it may not be perfect, but the spiritual love and hard work that we've placed into it can never be replaced. We have no choice but to do our best to be committed, to be faithful, to work together, and to be patient through the tough and confusing times. Abraham and Sarah experienced real life struggles of dealing with patience during tough and confusing times. While they were called Abram and Sarai, they had been impatient and confusion was in the midst of them. Sarai wanted a child, as did Abram. Sarai had what she thought was a clever idea to use one of her servants to be somewhat of a surrogate to her and Abram. That confusion led to emotions being lost in a union of a man and woman. But what the Lord did was turn that confusion into a blessing. When Abram was 99 years old, the Lord paid him a visit, He told *Abram:*

1 I am God Almighty; walk before me faithfully and be blameless. 2 Then I will make my covenant between me and you and will greatly increase your numbers.
Genesis 17:1-2 NIV

The scripture then goes on to say, **5 No longer will you be called Abram; your name will be Abraham, for I have made you a father of many nations.** What was even more interesting was the next step within this covenant that's correcting the impatience. Scriptures says in *Genesis 17:15-16,* **As for Sarai your wife, you are no longer to call her Sarai; her name will be Sarah. 16 I will bless her and will surely give you a son by her. I will bless her so that she will be the mother of nations; kings of peoples will come from her.**

Marriage isn't easy; there will always be a bit of confusion, tough times, and yes, your patience will be tried. We've had several instances where we got so frustrated and impatient, that we were at points where we wanted to throw in the towel. How would that have benefited the future for our children? How would that have benefited us as a family? If we would have given up due to being impatient, how would that correlate with saving the family and working together? In those moments, what we did was get on our knees, and prayed together. And we asked the Lord to fix it. Because after all, a family that prays together, stays together.

If we, as men and women, husbands and wives, loving and engaged courting couples, can't humble ourselves to be virtuous together and to have spiritual strength, to have faith, and patience, then the above scripture will be null and void. If we can simply work together as a family and continuously ask the Lord to fix our spiritual lives and put in the must needed work, imagine how strong we would be. Our families will be reinforced and there would be an increase in communication, faith, and patience. Peace and love will be in the home with spiritual protection of the family. Behind every Godly man, there is indeed a Godly woman. We've all heard this all too often. As most couples do, we celebrate our anniversary; we've been married for 8 years, but we have been together since high school. We went through hell and back as young teenagers trying to make a relationship happen when those surrounding us said, "You have your whole life to find your true love". Throughout our relationship, it hasn't been easy and we still encounter struggles now and then. It's only by God's grace and mercy, prayer, and faithfulness, that He has allowed us to continue our relationship by working together and depending on Him as we continuously hollered, "Fix it Lord, Fix it!"

III
EXTRAORDINARY PEOPLE

25 Now there was a man in Jerusalem called Simeon, who was righteous and devout. He was waiting for the consolation of Israel, and the Holy Spirit was on him. 26 It had been revealed to him by the Holy Spirit that he would not die before he had seen the Lord's Messiah. 27 Moved by the Spirit, he went into the temple courts. When the parents brought in the child Jesus to do for him what the custom of the Law required, 28 Simeon took him in his arms and praised God, saying: 29 "Sovereign Lord, as you have promised, you may now dismiss your servant in peace. 30 For my eyes have seen your salvation, 31 which you have prepared in the sight of all nations: 32 a light for revelation to the Gentiles, and the glory of your people Israel.
Luke 2:25-32 NIV

According to the 2016 United States Census Bureau, we have an estimated population of 323,000,000 people in the United States; a little over one-third of this population is comprised of newborns. This breaks down to at least 4.2 births every second. With the birth of each baby, family and friends are crowded in the waiting rooms. Husbands and significant others are excited, nervous, elated, and ready to cut the umbilical cord and to see the loving face and blessing of a son or daughter. Friends and family await at home or at work to hear the good news of the weight, the length, and the name. Pastors or family spiritual leaders await the opportunity to present the child in obedience to the Lord. During these moments, everyone is typically excited because of what the future has in store for the newborn baby. In the gospel of Luke 2:25-32, I've studied the story of how the excitement of Jesus had slowly spread throughout the land. We know of the Magi; most of us may know them as "the wise men" that have traveled from far because of this star which has appeared in the night sky. Simeon, whom I'll further expound upon within this book, waits with patience, faith, and trust in the Holy Spirit!

The focal points will be of those very actions taken by Simeon as his excitement level and anticipation was endless as he yearned to see the loving face of our Savior. It would be the face of a baby unlike no other, a baby whose existence is astonishing beyond belief. Furthermore, it would be a baby who exudes the aura of being extraordinary to all people.

2 Speak to the sons of Israel, saying, when a woman gives birth and bears a male child, then she shall be unclean for seven days, as in the days of her menstruation she shall be unclean".
Leviticus 12:2 NIV

It was customary for the mother to go through a purification process. Mary, with the support of Joseph, was simply fulfilling the duties as any strong parent would at that time; it was a part of their custom in obedience to the Lord. In addition, according to the Jewish custom, the male child would be circumcised on the eighth day, and on that day, the name Jesus was given to the child—the name the angel gave him before his conception. In the custom of purification, there were strict directives in accordance with the laws set forth. The mother could not touch anything sacred, nor go to the sanctuary until the days of purification was over. When the purification was over for Mary, she and Joseph took Jesus to Jerusalem to the Temple. If you cannot visualize the temple in those days, it is equivalent to what we think of now as Mega churches. You see this too was written in the law that every firstborn male child be consecrated and go through a sacred dedication to the Lord. Also, they were to offer up a sacrifice of a pair of doves or two pigeons. You see the fact that the child Jesus was indeed the Savior didn't stop him from receiving the proper, natural upbringing. Jesus was to be raised as any other child in the Jewish custom, and those specific steps were taken to ensure that he would be raised to know and understand the Lord. While in the Temple, there was a humble, righteous, and devout man named Simeon. Most would say that Simeon was a Priest or even a Sanhedrin, but the scripture describes him by specifically using the word "Devout", to purposely let us know that Simeon was deeply religious and committed to the Lord. Simeon had been waiting on this "consolation of Israel" or this bright and shining star who was said to be the Savior of all nations. With this wait, this display of patience, the Holy Spirit was said to be on him. Verse 26 of the scripture reads,

26…the Holy Spirit revealed to him that he would not die before he had seen the Lord's Messiah.
Luke 2:26 NIV

So, we are now at the point where this revealing would finally come to pass. As Mary and Joseph brought Jesus into the Temple, they were met by Simeon. My question to you, as the reader, is how did Simeon know they would be at the Temple? The scripture says that Simeon was led. The Holy Spirit led him to the Temple courts. Take some time after this message and think to yourself, has the Holy Spirit ever led you somewhere or to do something?

When my family and I moved to Daytona Beach, FL our first spiritual mission was to find a church suitable for all of us. As an intern at Bethune-Cookman University (B-CU) in 2012, I attended a couple of churches in the area. My family was still residing in Illinois. The churches I visited in Daytona Beach were indeed nurturing and Christ was in the midst.

However, that was only good enough for me individually. The following year, I was offered a position at B-CU. My family and I drove from the Midwest to the Deep South to start this new endeavor in our lives. We went to the churches that I had visited a year ago; however, they weren't a good fit for us as a family. In that moment, our patience was truly being tested. We yearned for a church family and home so instantaneously that it frustrated us. It frustrated us because it wasn't coming together as fast as we wanted it to. My family and I then prayed together and asked God to send us to a spiritual space where we could be nurtured and fed with the Word.

We were then led by the Holy Spirit to Historic New Bethel AME of Ormond Beach, FL. This commute took only 15 minutes from campus. I remember it like it was yesterday as my family and I walked into the sanctuary during Sunday school. The first person that approached us was Pastor Reginald B. Johnson, Sr. (pastor at the time). He was so welcoming and hospitable. We grew a long lasting personal and spiritual relationship from that point on. When we returned home, my wife and I talked and came to the same conclusion that Historic New Bethel AME was going to be our new spiritual home. And this was due to us having continual faith, amid being impatient.

The Holy Spirit led Simeon to recognize this baby as the Savior. I believe Mary and Joseph felt a special anointing when meeting Simeon. Believe it or not, this happens even today just as the Holy Spirit led us to the church doors in Ormond Beach.

Once a child is born and that baby is taken to the church, everybody wants to hold the baby, whether it's to feel the loving warmth or to simply speak blessings upon him or her. What happened at the temple wasn't uncommon. However, there was an extraordinary event that did occur. When Simeon took Jesus in his arms he gave a song of praise to God:

29 Sovereign Lord, as you have promised, you may now dismiss[d] your servant in peace 30 For my eyes have seen your salvation, 31 which you have prepared in the sight of all nations: 32 a light for revelation to the Gentiles, and the glory of your people Israel.
Luke 2:29-32 NIV

At that point, the Holy Spirit was truly at work. This is how the Holy Spirit operates for us as believers. It communicates with us and guides us; it is here for us as a tool to persevere in times where we find confusion. Think of a time where you were driving in an unfamiliar place and got lost and frustration started to arise. Instead of fussing and cussing, you call on the Lord for help! The Holy Spirit hears you, and with trust and belief in it, it enters in as an unknown functional being and guides you to your destination, or to someone more than willing to assist you. Situations such as this can't be anything but the Lord himself. Think again about a time when you couldn't pay a bill, or there wasn't enough food for the family, and pay day was more than a week away. Again, instead of fussing and cussing, you call on the Lord for help. The Lord hears you, and with the trust and belief that you should possess, the Holy Spirit enters yet again to guide and place you where you need to be. After Simeon praised God for what was promised to him, and after Mary and Joseph were amazed at this anointed spirit-driven blessing, he then went on to explain to Mary and Joseph of yet another promise or prophetic moment:

34 Simeon blessed them and said to Mary, his mother: "This child is destined to cause the falling and rising of many in Israel, and to be a sign that will be spoken against, 35 so that the thoughts of many hearts will be revealed. And a sword will pierce your own soul too.
Luke 2:34-35 NIV

This baby who was said to be the Light and Salvation; this innocent baby Jesus was said to be the cause of great joy but also grave despair. Scripture specifically says there will be the rise and falling of many in Israel, of all nations. There were many thoughts and hearts that were revealed! Many said to themselves, is this the true Messiah? Our true Savior? Is this the one who was sent by our God? But others marveled in belief, with confidence that he is the one. We have to remember he didn't appear in a manner that was extravagant to the eyes; he didn't ascend from the skies on clouds with music and harps being played. He came into this world just like you and me. As we all may know, when Jesus got older and his calling flourished, he ran into two types of people. I call them R&R, but not the common meaning of rest and relaxation. He ran into people who were either receptive or rejecting; in other words, people either were receptive in believing who he is or rejected the entire notion of his very existence.

When it comes to believing, there is no neutral ground. Lastly, in this prophetic interaction between Simeon and Jesus; he said to Mary **"a sword will pierce your own soul too."** After Mary gave birth to Jesus, after raising Jesus, after hearing and witnessing the good, bad, and the ugly, and after enduring everything her son had gone through, she then endured the pain of witnessing his worldly death. And as she witnessed him upon the cross as a spear pierced his side, it also pierced her soul. Mary dealt with this pain, the anguish of his sacrifice upon the cross. This was the prophecy of Simeon. As he gave his prophecy to Mary and Joseph, a prophetess approached to witness and to also be in the midst of Jesus. The prophetess was Anna. Anna also possessed faith and trust in the Holy Spirit; she had also been known as a faithful and devout woman of The Lord. An eighty-four-year-old widow, she had been well in age just as Simeon. Anna had been a strong worshipper at the temple on a consistent basis, fasting and praying daily. Her relationship with The Lord was known to be impeccable! Anna approached our Savior as he was an infant.

38 She gave thanks to God and spoke about the child to all who were looking forward to the redemption of Jerusalem.
Luke 2:38 NIV

Led by the Holy Spirit, she spoke blessings of Jesus and thanked God for his arrival. She too was privileged to be one of the first to see the face of our Messiah.

I believe Simeon held strongly to the three points that I've described throughout this message of patience, faith, and trust in the Holy Spirit. The belief in all three is the same that an ill bedridden father or mother would lean on when wanting to see the face of his or her son, daughter, grandchildren, and loved ones before what he or she thinks may be his or her last days. To possess these very few components gives one spiritual strength because when doing this, it's giving God the glory and the power. If you too believe Christ, and believe in having patience, faith, and trust in the Holy Spirit, it too will continuously give you spiritual strength. You too will then be giving Him glory and power and receive abundant blessings.

IV
SPIRITUAL SIGHT

1 As he went along, he saw a man blind from birth. 2 His disciples asked him, "Rabbi, who sinned, this man or his parents, that he was born blind?" 3 "Neither this man nor his parents sinned," said Jesus, "but this happened so that the works of God might be displayed in him. 4 As long as it is day, we must do the works of him who sent me. Night is coming, when no one can work. 5 While I am in the world, I am the light of the world." 6 After saying this, he spit on the ground, made some mud with the saliva, and put it on the man's eyes. 7 "Go," he told him, "wash in the Pool of Siloam" (this word means "Sent"). So the man went and washed, and came home seeing.
John 9:1-7 NIV

For several years now, even before I answered the call to preach God's Word, I've had a sermon placed upon my heart, a message that I felt needed to be heard. There were certain behaviors that I've noticed in people, family members, friends, and even my own son at a very early age. These behaviors were like signs that I believe the Lord has given us as His children, as His disciples to assure us of His daily presence. We, as Christians, as believers, are able to see through what's known as spiritual eyes—an anointed behavior that He has blessed us with. While getting my visual and mental breaks by way of scrolling through social media, a friend of mine posted a status that she was jogging. She said she turned a corner while running and saw a tree. She made it clear and plain by telling us as readers what she had noticed. Others may have seen that tree for what was, but that particular tree was in a certain shape, unlike others, the shape of a cross. I then ran across another friend's Facebook page and she posted a picture and mentioned that she saw a tow truck. To anyone else, they may have just seen that truck for what it was. But she noticed that the lift that picks up and positions the vehicles was in the shape of a cross. This message comes from the book of John, chapter 9, where Jesus gave sight to a blind man. Here's a question and thought for you as the reader, how does one receive spiritual sight?

There are three steps that I want to offer you in helping you receive your spiritual sight. The first of the three is to accept. Accepting circumstances out of the norm.

2 His disciples asked him, "Rabbi, who sinned, this man or his parents, that he was born blind?" 3 "Neither this man nor his parents sinned," said Jesus.
John 9:2-3 NIV

If we, in fact, want to see through spiritual eyes, we must accept and not resist signs that are in our plain sight daily. We can't think that the perfect stranger who simply says good morning and extends his right hand is "doing too much." We cannot assume that our colleague in the next cubical or the teacher in class is prying for information when she senses that you're not having a good day. When we accept those kind gestures from others who seem genuinely concerned, we almost always must know that it's an extension of the love and kindness which cometh from the Lord. It's a form of His communication towards us. Remember and recognize that He communicates with us through the Word, people, the spirit, and through different life encounters when you least expect it. I believe we should all be open to accepting spiritual circumstances which are out of the norm.

Do you believe that everything happens for a reason? Let's look at verse 3, it reads, **this happened so that the works of God might be displayed in him.**

A wise Pastor once told me that we may be either going into a storm; we may already be in a storm; or we may be coming out of a storm. In other words, we're always transitioning. In the case of the blind man, his storm happened to be his sight and he had been in this storm all of his life, since birth. We too also can be blind. We go through storms so that we can be a witness of God's miraculous works. Being open to accepting circumstances out of the norm is important and it is essential in many ways. For example, we should accept kind gestures. I don't know your story, but I can definitely testify about mine and how I had to go through something to persevere. I knew that I had to crawl before I walked, or at least that's what I was always told. Essentially, I went through an experience to help me grow.

Throughout this book, I will be vulnerable in telling you how my life was and how, at one point in time, I stood in the dark. I've gone through experiences such as drinking alcohol and smoking weed religiously to partying and neglecting my responsibilities. At that time in my life, I was truly blind. When were you blind? What did you do to gain or recover spiritual sight? One step in getting your spiritual sight is by accepting circumstances. You see, Jesus has this unwavering confidence, He told us what's impossible but then went against the odds by showing us how the impossible can be defied.

4 As long as it is day, we must do the works of him who sent me. Night is coming, when no one can work. 5 While I am in the world, I am the light of the world.
John 9:4-5 NIV

Jesus is the light of the world. What he is telling us is that we need to have faith. This is the second step in gaining spiritual sight, having faith. When we go to the doctor, whether it's because of a common cold, inherited health issues, or any type of emergency, what is it that we hold on to? It is faith because if we didn't have the faith that we would be healed then we wouldn't go in the first place. When we come into God's church, what is it that we hold on to? Isn't it a spiritual healing that we are looking for? And one thing that comes along with that healing is faith. Think about that for a minute. Think about faith being the second step in gaining your spiritual sight. We've heard the biblical story time after time about Job and how he lost his livestock, workers, and even his children in this unknown communication with the Lord and Satan. Do we truly apply Job's lessons in our lives? If a man can lose his earthly riches, his business, and his children to the hands of the adversary, and still have faith, that within itself should be a testament in how we should live daily. Faith can take us a long way.

Moses accepted and had faith. Abraham accepted and had faith. Shadrach, Meshach, and Abednego accepted and had faith. They accepted the light and had faith in the light. What would give us the right to *not* accept and have faith? We see His works done every day. Yes, there is war; yes, there is racism; and yes, there are injustices. The world isn't perfect, but if we accept and have faith we will learn, know, and understand that we may be in this world, but we are not of this world. When you possess spiritual sight, you *know* that you're on a completely different level than others.

This blind man accepted who Christ was, and then took another step in having trusting faith that Christ, who was a stranger at the time, could give him sight. How many of us can say we can do that today? How many of us can run into a situation where your lights get cut off and lose our job,

34

all while having hungry children at home? Will you hold on to faith? Will you trust Christ? Will you trust the stranger that comes to you and says, "God is with you"? Because that stranger could be one of the strongest stakeholders in a small church that can get your lights turned back on! That stranger could be a manager and can bless you with a job! You see according to scripture, a lot of us need to re-evaluate the way we encounter others. Have faith and recognize the light of the world because the more we do this, the more we will notice more signs along the path of gaining spiritual sight.

6 After saying this, he spits on the ground, made some mud with the saliva, and put it on the man's eyes.
John 9:6 NIV

At this point, the blind man believed. How many of us would let someone spit on the ground and gather mud to be placed on us or our child? How many of us would let a stranger touch us or our child? To believe is the third step in receiving spiritual sight. The blind man had accepted Jesus, gained faith in Jesus, and as I believe was led by the Holy Spirit because he had then fully believed in Jesus who could then give him the sight that he'd yearned for. I've had many nights where I had to accept different circumstances, have faith, and believed that certain situations would give me the insight of where I should be or what I should do. I remember those days as a young adult not having a job and living with my mother again. I remember those days where I had too much pride which led me to be unemployed, where no one wanted to work with me. Jesus told the blind man,

7 "Go," he told him, "wash in the Pool of Siloam" (this word means "Sent"). So the man went and washed, and came home seeing.
John 9:7 NIV

Jesus then told the blind man to wash in fresh water. He wanted the blind man to make himself clean. And once he did this, by way of accepting, having faith, and believing, he was given sight. He then went to be washed and cleaned and was then unrecognizable. He went home and indeed, no one recognized the blind man who could now see. You see once he cleaned himself from all the blemish, grime, and dirt that caused him to be blind, he was then able to see.

When we wash ourselves now in the sanctified water, after we've accepted, gained faith, and believed in Christ's miraculous works, there's no limit to what we can see and accomplish once we've gained spiritual sight. And even with that, other people will see us in a different light,
Hallelujah! You would think that familiar people may know us, but they won't because we are unrecognizable. We would be so clean that no one would recognize us because we walk differently, talk differently, and operate differently in the newness of life.

If you have yet to read the book of John, I advise you to do so. It is truly an eye opener (pun intended). As it is written in scripture, **whether he is a sinner or not, I don't know. One thing I do know. I was blind now I see!**

V
PROMISES FROM GOD: PEACE & LEGACY (LASTING LEGACY)

As I stood in the pulpit for one of my monthly sermons in the absence of our Pastor, all I could think about was the pressure of having to invoke the Holy Spirit in the midst of a spiritual warfare which plagued our nation. I started out thanking God for all he has done and brought us through, and then thanked the church members, minister, and ministries. One thing I feel should be accomplished daily is praying for others and as many people as you can possibly think of. Whether you are fond of them or not, pray for a blessing upon them in a mighty way along with grace and mercy; it all correlates to our inner peace. To meditate and thank our Father for continual peace is part of his promise to us. This message will speak to a burning topic that has been within me for some time.

Amid this world's confusion, we find ourselves at war with each other, at war in the community, and in a racial war that's not confined by a majority located in the southern states anymore. We are in a spiritual and political war, and other countries are probably laughing and sitting back in their La-Z-Boys watching us kill each other and kill the innocent. I'm angry and saddened, and as brave as most may think I am, I also experience fear.

During a theater production in the summer of 2016, I gathered with several people from my immediate community of all races and ages, men and women. We formed a circle together and had a moment of silence for the tragic loss of two African American men and 5 officers whose lives were taken due to the adversary's hate. In this circle after a moment of silence, the option was given to all those who were willing to give words of encouragement and their thoughts about what had happened. Naturally, I was the first to step forward to share my thoughts and feelings. I felt God had placed several words upon my heart to share in the aftermath of what the world had literally and visually witnessed. I shared with the circle, at that time, that we aren't even one year away from the loss of Sister Sandra Bland. I shared with the circle that it's not just our brothers who are in danger, but our sisters are as well. It is now being spewed in the media of how hate affects Native Americans and Latinos as well. I shared with this circle how I am in fear when driving to work, or driving home. I shared with this circle that I have two sons who do not yet fully understand the evils of the world, but I am hopeful and prayerful that they don't fall short of it. The most important message I shared with this circle is that if I were to ever fall victim to the evils of the world, that I leave an optimistic and lasting legacy. I would like others to know about all of the things that I have been doing by leading spiritually, mentoring, role modeling, educating, inspiring, etc. and that it has not been in vain. Focusing on two scriptures and two topical points: *Navigating Spiritually through Confusion* (Romans 12:9-19) and *Leaving a Positive Spiritual Legacy* (2 Timothy 4:2-5).

9 Love must be sincere. Hate what is evil; cling to what is good. 10 Be devoted to one another in love. Honor one another above yourselves. 11 Never be lacking in zeal, but keep your spiritual fervor, serving the Lord.
Romans 12:9-11 NIV

Everything we've witnessed during the summer of 2016 came with a side of confusion and no balance. That is where we are as a society, as Americans, and especially as Christians as we all search for common ground. In the midst of confusion and not having a balance in society, we are lacking love and are falling short of the ways of the world little by little. It's as if we are either combatting evil with evil or condoning hate with hate, it is our human nature to be this way. Here's the caveat: The Lord steps in to remind us every so often through scripture in Romans 12:9-11 that it is in our best interest to kill the adversary with kindness. What if I told you that it is actually possible to live in peace through all turmoil? As I write this message, it reminds me of the movie Rosewood when the Preacher of an AME church attempted to reach a member of the congregation through a spiritual approach, the member then vocalized with anger and said: "I ain't in no praying mood preacha." I want to circle back to what that character stated. I want you to know that you better be in a praying and spiritual meditating mood *always*. Praying is one of the strongest weapons that a believer can possess. There's power in the name of Jesus. If you truly believe in Christ, then you will know that this time deserves prayer, now, more than ever before. When one has faith, we can talk to God asking for guidance in all that happens daily. He then communicates to you through His infinite avenues letting you know that He will always be there.

As history continues to repeat itself, I notice that there are more peaceful protests being organized in different places throughout the country, and even the world. I too have also supported different movements by taking part in them. Like prayer, these protests will all be in vain if there is no action. I tell my students this all the time that protesting is good, do it as often as you can to show that you are demanding change. But, protesting, just like prayer, cannot be the only and end result. Seeing the results in these protests just as seeing the results in your prayers will require you to put work and action into effect.

2 Preach the word; be prepared in season and out of season; correct, rebuke and encourage – with great patience and careful instruction. 3 For the time will come when people will not put up with sound doctrine. Instead, to suit their own desires, they will gather around them a great number of teachers to say what their itching ears want to hear. 4 They will turn their ears away from the truth and turn aside to myths. 5 But you, keep your head in all situations, endure hardship, do the work of an evangelist, discharge all the duties of your ministry.
2 Timothy 4:2-5 NIV

Verse 5 in the above scripture exhibits the type of spiritual leadership I would like to leave as an example for my sons and daughter, those who I am a role model for and mentor, and those whom I lead holistically. To be prepared in season and out of season means that one must always be prepared for all battles. Having the integrity to correct oneself and others, to admonish negativity, and to encourage friends, neighbors, and even those who may have your least interest at hand. One must realize and understand that this process won't be easy and recognize that it will take a cool and calm demeanor. Spiritual leadership is the legacy I yearn to leave behind. I want for those who I leave a spiritual legacy with to always keep a level head, to be loving, to be understanding, and to have compassion. Know that Christ can provide the desires of the heart only to those who believe. 2 Timothy 4:2-5 also speaks to those who possess a worldly character and those who are easily angered, foolish, ignorant, conspiracy theorist, and evolution believers. Be careful of who you choose to linger in your inner circle. The world is filled with teachers and differing doctrine. The world is filled with individuals who feel like they possess all the answers. I challenge you to challenge them with solid spiritual apologetics. Be careful to not turn away from the truth, only to make yourself vulnerable to generational mythologies.

Navigating spiritually through confusion and leaving a positive spiritual legacy are two essential components in reshaping your immediate surrounding and community. Moving forward, I urge you to adhere to the following: Know that the easily angered lacks training, and shoot at the innocent. Think about the countless fathers, sons, brothers, and cousins whose lives were taken due to individuals whom were easily anger and lacked training. And now, mothers, daughters, and sisters are condemned just the same. The world and its history have truly repeated itself. The foolish and ignorant are easily persuaded and retaliate or think about retaliation. These have been proven so due to the killing of law enforcement, the very entity whom we deem to protect us. Those who lack belief and subject themselves to foolish and ignorant thoughts taint the mission of those who are genuine and are well trained to protect us. We must remove ourselves from combating hate with hate.

The conspiracy theorists and evolution believers place Christ in the back seat of the Cadillac. Judging would contradict the entire essence of this text, but I believe in Christ Jesus. To indulge in conspiracy theories and believing in evolution only places you in a position to straddle the fence, so to speak. When believing in Christ, know that you are either on one side or the other.

If we carefully read and indulge ourselves in scripture, it will slowly be revealed what the Lord wants for us. It is God's promise to us, but only if you believe. How do you intend on leaving a positive spiritual legacy amid all confusion? How do you plan to navigate spiritually through confusion?

This message is dedicated to the families of those who lost their loved ones to excessive police brutality.

Family

My loving mother Dolorese Grant-Fall.

My grandparents, Stephenson Grant (Deceased) and Claudia Grant.
They are the foundation of our large family.

My siblings: Pierre Grant, Myself, Nkrumah Grant, Khadim Fall, Courtisha
Grant, and Khoudia Fall

Spirituality

September 30, 2012, I was baptized by Reverend Charlie B. Cross.

My trial sermon in February of 2013 at Bethel African Methodist Episcopal Church – Carbondale, IL.

Reverend Reginald Johnson, Myself, and Reverend Willie Branch, in Orlando, FL at the 2013 11th District African Methodist Episcopal Annual Conference.

Reverend Larry D. Lewis, Sister Ruth Lathum, and I at Bethel African Methodist Episcopal Church – Champaign after service.

Education

Dr. Saran Donahoo of Southern Illinois University Carbondale has always been a nurturer. She was my best collegiate advisor by far. Getting ready to walk across the stage to receive my Master of Science degree in Education.

Everyone needs a mentor. Father Joseph Brown of Southern Illinois University Carbondale gave me a sense of peace navigating through tough battles during graduate school. I thank him dearly.

A couple of my mentors entering the field of Higher Education whom I will forever be grateful to and who have guided me. Crasha Townsend and Dr. Tasha Toy.

"History Always Repeats itself" –Willie E. Thompson (Deceased). A phrase he always taught us as his students at Delta College.

I was blessed to have the opportunity to travel to Ghana, West Africa in the summer of 2012. It was an amazing life changing experience traveling abroad during graduate school.

Community

Humble beginnings, St. Nicholas Housing Projects located in Harlem USA. I grew up here until the age of 13. Each year, I make a visit back to remind myself of how far I've come.

Protest/march in Champaign. IL. It has always been an innate character of mine to speak up for those who are oppressed. This protest was in the aftermath of Black and Brown men and women senselessly killed by excessive law enforcement.

We all stand on the shoulders of others. At First Ward Community Center with Azola Williams and Fred Harvey.

Saginaw Alumni Chapter of Kappa Alpha Psi Fraternity, Inc. (2010)

Recipient for 2017 Neighborhood-Community Building Star Award, by the City of Champaign Neighborhood Services Advisory Board. Past Champaign County NAACP President Patricia Avery and I.

Recipient for Central Illinois Business magazine's 10th Annual Forty under 40 award 2017, based on achievements, innovation, leadership ability, and expertise in one's chosen field and community. Family friend Mary Haywood-Benson and I.

Altruism and collaboration: Supporting Flint, MI by collecting and donating bottled water to Northridge Academy. (2016)
Chevez Marshall, Tekita Bankhead, Myself, Laura Hamilton, Dwarne McNair, Sr.

Family

My support system and source that keep pushing me towards creating a legacy. My wife Mallory Robertson. Sons, Jeremiah and Isaiah Robertson. (2017)

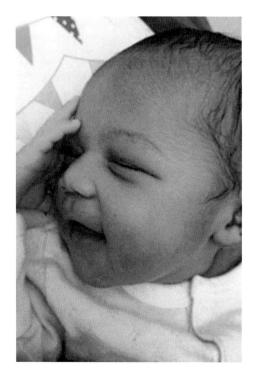

Our newest addition, our daughter, Danielle Barbara Robertson. Born September 22, 2017. Named after my best friend Daniel Smothers and Mother-in-law Barabara Jean Craion, both of whom have passed on to be with the Lord.

My childhood friend Daniel D. Smothers. (Deceased). He left a major, positive impact upon my life.

Another one of my childhood friends, Ardayell Brewer, who is more like a big brother. An unbreakable bond.

VI
HOW STRONG IS YOUR FAITH?

20 At this, Job got up and tore his robe and shaved his head. Then he fell to the ground in worship "Naked I came from my mother's womb, and naked I will depart. [c] The LORD gave and the LORD has taken away; may the name of the LORD be praised." 22 In all this, Job did not sin by charging God with wrongdoing.
Job 1:20-22 NIV

Job said, "In all this" What does that mean? How can our lives relate to Job? My attempt is to deliver a transparent message through the testimony of what Job went through and how we too go through similar daily tests. Job was said to be a man who was blameless, and upright. A story of a man that seems to have everything one can possibly imagine. Just imagine functioning daily and having an unwavering sense of security, no financial worries or burdens, the feeling of knowing that your health is fully in tack, and the feeling of knowing that your children and loved ones are always safe. Then imagine how all of this can be taken away in just the blink of an eye. I think it's safe for us all to agree that there have been one or more trying situations that have happened in our lives—situations that are so traumatic that it's left us mentally crippled. It is with that crippled state of mind that leads to the very question that I use as the title of this message. "How Strong Is Your Faith?"

6 One day the angels came to present themselves before the Lord,

and Satan also came with them. 7 The Lord said to Satan, "Where have you come from?"
Job 1:6-7 NIV

The Lord and Satan were having somewhat of a contest. There was a certain dialogue going on, an actual conversation. It is during this conversation that the Lord is concerned with only two things. When the angels were presenting themselves to the Lord, it just so happened that Satan was right along with them. The angels were presenting themselves, not even knowing that Satan was in their very presence.

7 The Lord said to Satan, "Where have you come from?" Satan answered the Lord, "From roaming throughout the earth, going back and forth on it." 8 Then the Lord said to Satan, "Have you considered my servant Job? There is no one on earth like him; he is blameless and upright, a man who fears God and shuns evil.
Job 1:7-8 NIV

Satan had permission to go back and forth. So, it wasn't uncommon for him to be in places where he wasn't welcome. It's not uncommon now because as we all know, he could be sitting or standing next to you at this very moment. It was almost as if the Lord knew what Satan had brought himself up there for. You see, just like many of us, Job is getting ready to go through several situations to test his reliance and devotion to God. A lot of times when we're going through tough situations, we're going through them for a reason unknown to us. For example, you're having car trouble, although you've just purchased a full-service oil change, and the car is in great shape. Every day you leave 8:30 am sharp, it just so happens on that day you've left at 8:45 am; tragically there has been an accident around the corner along your daily route. What if you had left at your usual time? Know that God placed you in that very situation to be late and have car trouble. Or what about a weekend trip that's been planned for months? In this case, your finances didn't come through on the Friday that it's normally deposited into your account. You now don't have the funds in time to make that trip that you had planned for months, so you had to miss out. But on Monday afternoon, those finances appeared. Tuesday afternoon an unexpected, financial situation occurs. If you would have gone out the past weekend, you wouldn't have had the funds to pay for what was needed. A lot of times when we're going through situations, we're going through them for a reason. God places us where he wants us to be, and we'll never know the reasoning behind His plan!

Job had gone through a multitude of tests because Satan was convinced that Job is only obedient because of the riches that he possesses. Does that sound familiar? Satan is dead locked on the fact that if these riches and possessions were taken away then Job's faith in the Lord would diminish. So, here's what's done to counteract Satan's ridiculous accusations. Satan was given the permission from the Lord to experiment with Job's loyalty, but throughout this, Satan was not to lay one finger on Job.

13 One day when Job's sons and daughters were feasting and drinking wine at the oldest brother's house, 14 a messenger came to Job and said, "The oxen were plowing and the donkeys were grazing nearby, 15 and the Sabeans attacked and made off with them. They put the servants to the sword, and I am the only one who has escaped to tell you!
Job 1:13-15 NIV

The oxen were very viable animals and tools. They were hard working, reliable, and they could be trained. They were plowing; the donkeys were doing their job tending to the grass and herbage. You have to understand that these were his tools for his business. Today, farmers use tractors, fertilizer, plows, and other innovative machinery to assist in the field. With this striking from Satan, Job's business was now in jeopardy. If you've ever met a successful business owner, the last thing you want to do is mess with his or her money. The last thing you want to do is mess with anyone's money; just think about how you would feel if you received the wrong change back. Job's property, tools, and livestock were carried off and to add further insult, his servants and workers were killed. Imagine having to go to the families of your employees to explain the death of their loved one. Understand that this was only test #1. While conversing with the first messenger another messenger came to Job.

16 While he was still speaking, another messenger came and said, "The fire of God fell from the heavens and burned up the sheep and the servants, and I am the only one who has escaped to tell you! Job 1:16 NIV

When we look at just these two situations, we may say to ourselves, what a day endured by Job. After just losing one set of livestock and a viable part of his business, he was struck, yet, again. How many times have you just wanted to break down? How many times have you felt you had no one or nowhere to turn to? How many times have you felt you didn't know what to do and you're at a standstill? Just think about a time when you felt this way. When you're in that mood, it's like something must be done immediately to fix or heal the situation. I, too, have personally been in a similar situation, and what I did was locate that inner faith and prayed for strength knowing that God will guide me through.

You see Satan's main goal was to break Job's spirit; his main goal is to break your spirit and to make a point and prove to our God that faith isn't real. Look at the tactical moves Satan attempted and used against Job to break him down. Look at the commonalities of what was taken away. Satan thought if he took away what was thought to be Job's most precious possessions then he would lose his sight on God. Understand that this happens in everyday life. Businesses go bankrupt; stock markets crash while billions of dollars are lost. We witness how people succumb to alcohol, drugs, and committing suicide. Think about how those feelings align with Job's, and where his mindset was at that very moment. While Job was still speaking, another messenger came to him.

17 While he was still speaking, another messenger came and said, "The Chaldeans formed three raiding parties and swept down on your camels and made off with them. They put the servants to the sword, and I am the only one who has escaped to tell you!
Job 1:17 NIV

So far, we have three incidents with three commonalities. There were three attempts to break Job's moral and his faith. His services and resources were basically wiped out. Times like these would probably bring about old-time phrases that we always hear our parents or grandparents say when there are situations of trial and distress. Phrases such as, "If it ain't one thing it's another;" "I can't win, for losing;" "When the going gets tough the tough get going;" and the most common, "When it rains, it pours". You see Satan is cleverer than we think he is; he knows that without faith, there is fear. He knows that faith and fear are perfect opposites. At this point, Job's faith wasn't as strong as it was in the end of his journey. Job's business was one of his most important assets aside from his children. His business not only provided for him and his family, it also provided an opportunity for employment and community. Job's children were the priority; he prayed for them daily with burnt offerings. So there had to have been a fear of either losing his business and or his children. Once he let that fear in and left his faith unguarded, he left open a door for Satan to come in. You see faith is like a shield, but you must believe in it, God promises to shield us, but we must believe. If you let that belief fade, fear and doubt enter into your lives. Satan enters with all intentions to kill, steal, and destroy. So, now we've had Job converse with three messengers who have brought him word that his business has been shattered. His livestock, servants, services, and resources were all stolen or killed. While dealing with this news another messenger came to him.

18 While he was still speaking, yet another messenger came and said, "Your sons and daughters were feasting and drinking wine at the oldest brother's house, 19 when suddenly a mighty wind swept in from the desert and struck the four corners of the house. It collapsed on them and they are dead, and I am the only one who has escaped to tell you!
Job 1:18-19 NIV

During my high school years, I connected with a gentle soul that accepted me as nothing short of his brother. This young anointed youth and I played sports together, had classes together, shared clothes, and hung out daily; this goes to show you how close we were. As a native of Harlem, NYC and only being in Saginaw, MI, at the time of getting acquainted, for a little over a year, I had no close friends and didn't desire to have any. This young teenager's name was Daniel Demond Smothers—now a household name in the City of Saginaw as one whose life was taken far too soon. He was a model son, grandson, brother, nephew, cousin, and mentor to many at a young age. Daniel was afforded such a bright future in which he worked so hard to gain. Being one of the physically smallest in his in-crowd, he obtained a huge, vibrant, loud, and loving personality to light up any room filled with darkness. I, among others, was afforded the opportunity to encounter and bond with Daniel, as he was used in this world to intrinsically motivate many. He was Christ fearing, fearless to challenges, but cautious and smart enough to know what it took to overcome trials while having faith. He'd always use a saying that I'd still quote today. When one was going through a trying situation he'd say, "Suck it up." Daniel sought to one day go on to play college football on a full ride scholarship and major in education—the very career that comes naturally to me. Helping people, that's how we were raised, with the character of altruism, always having selfless concern for the welfare of others. On January 1, 1999, Daniel's life was taken due to the cowardly acts of one who saw fit to use a fire arm to solve a dispute. Daniel was killed in a drive-by shooting. He lost his life in the presence of a close relative, and just like Job, the hope of many collapsed only to leave one to escape and tell what happened.

A while back, I spoke with Ms. Debry Smothers, Daniel's mother. I told her how I wanted to deliver a message to the masses on faith as it relates to the book of Job and to be a testament for many. She further proved to me how strong one's faith can be. She told me that anything she goes through is nothing compared to what she's going to get in the end. She told me she truly believes that God wouldn't put more on her than she couldn't bear. Of course, in the beginning, it was hard to believe what she said. Of course, she had people asking her why God didn't save Daniel?

She dealt with this real-life Job situation. A situation that one will never understand because it's not meant to be understood. By her being a God-fearing woman, she became devoted to the Christian life; she built her outlook on faith differently, and became stronger spiritually. She didn't result to alcohol, drugs, or prostitution; and she certainly didn't curse God. Her new intake on faith is what brought her through tribulations and trials and which still has her standing strong! Sometimes we go through so much that our friends out in the world would tell us anything.

As time went on, Sister Davis read the word of God, understood, and found a way to accept her situations. This unfortunate situation that was traumatic was turned into something of value. A scholarship was created in Daniel's name. She then went on to say that in the worldly eye you can't see things, but in the spiritual eye, you see more. The situations that she'd gone through was crippling, but she endured faithfully, and like Job, in the end, she gained double and triple because of those trials she has gone through. Sister Davis now has 2 grandsons, and through the closeness of our relationship, she also has Jeremiah, Isaiah, and Danielle (my daughter named after Daniel). She also has tons of nephews to add to her legacy.

Have faith! God has promised this to us; all we must do is believe. Along with this journey in gaining faith, Job learned endurance; it behooves us to do the same. When my family and I left Michigan for Illinois, we leaned on faith, but it wasn't as strong as it is now. We had to struggle, and with that struggle, we built and learned endurance; we learned to do away with fear. We channeled our inner Job. You too have a little Job inside of you, we all do. So, I ask you, how strong is your faith?

VII
RECEIVE YOUR CROWN OF GLORY

2 Be shepherds of God's flock that is under your care, watching over them—not because you must, but because you are willing, as God wants you to be; not pursuing dishonest gain, but eager to serve; 3 not lording it over those entrusted to you, but being examples to the flock. 4 And when the Chief Shepherd appears, you will receive the crown of glory that will never fade away.
I Peter 5:2-4 NIV

2 Tend (nurture, guard, guide, and fold) the flock of God that is [your responsibility], not by coercion or constraint, but willingly; not dishonorably motivated by the advantages and profits [belonging to the office], but eagerly and cheerfully; 3 Not domineering [as arrogant, dictatorial, and overbearing persons] over those in your charge, but being examples (patterns and models of Christian living) to flock (the congregation). 4 And [then] when the Chief Shepherd is revealed, you will win the conqueror's crown of glory.
I Peter 5:2-4 AMPC

A question was asked of me a while ago about if I ever get nervous when delivering messages of hope and faith. I explained that at times I do get nervous, and even though I feel I'm called to deliver His word, being nervous is a natural emotion. I stand on the shoulders of a very well-respected role model, Reverend Dr. Desmon Daniel. I could remember sitting in the church pews of Saginaw Bethel African Methodist Episcopal Church. As he approached the podium in the pulpit, he demanded attention as he invoked the Holy Spirit by singing his signature verse from Smokie

Norful's "I need you now". I witnessed how this man of God was used as a vessel to bring forth anointed messages to transform the masses. I then saw fit to emulate the same style, in hopes of continuing to breathe spiritual life into whomever I brought the message to. I learned that singing before bringing the message gave me a calming feeling and centered me. It placed me on a plateau where I could confidently deliver the words that had been given to me from our heavenly Father. As I sat on a Saturday night preparing this message, God had placed it upon my heart to entitle it "Receive your Crown of Glory", which derives from the fourth verse of the above scripture above.

Like Peter, the person I used to be and the man who I am now are like night and day. I used to be selfish, disrespectful, and didn't have my priorities in order. At a young age, ignoring the rearing of my mother, I abused alcohol, marijuana, and became a known womanizer. This led me to practice the undisciplined behaviors of becoming a cheater toward women and life. I used profane language daily (and still struggle with it at times), and I would always be negatively outspoken. I've since learned how to speak with caution; I can go on and on; my activities were said to be unbecoming. A wretch was what I was and still am at times. I was a person poor and unhappy in spirit. A lot of our youth today would confuse these antics by stating that they t-up! So, believe me when I say, I used to t-up. In fact, we had different sayings in the 90s and early 2000s. I grew up in the crowd that used to be "off the chain", then moved towards getting "crunk", then I messed around and got "hyped", and now youth of today get "t-up" and get "lit"!

After these immature phases of my life, I realized who Christ was and understood what he had done for me, just like Simon Peter—being obedient, humble, and choosing to follow Him in all I do. The Lord used Peter, a person who most people in the worldly eye also thought was unbecoming. Our heavenly creator saw fit that his one and only son Jesus mentored and used Peter so that he would use his attributes to reach multitudes then and now. Peter, who was also referred to as the Rock, the one who most would say was too brash, or outspoken turned out to be a teacher taught by the teacher.

My question to you within this message is how does one receive one's "Crown of Glory"? There are three scripturally based points I want to give you in preparing to receive it. The first is being submissive.

5 In the same, you who are younger, submit yourselves to your elders...
I Peter 5:5 NIV

We ask ourselves, what does it mean to be submissive? What does it mean to be submissive to those who are older? Within this letter that Peter has written, although it specifically reads to the elders (who were spiritual leaders of the early churches) and young men, I believe it is safe to say that this speaks to all men, women, and children. Everyone can identify if they've chosen to follow the teachings of Jesus Christ. Understand that during this time, Peter has chosen to submit himself, so he only wants us to be submissive as well (be submissive to those who are older). Peter chose to be submissive to Christ, a being who exudes an extremely high spiritual cognizance. Understand that nothing has changed from then to now; we too must learn how to be submissive daily. What we want to do is take it a bit further by praying daily, being kind and caring to one another, being respectful and concerned, and having compassion for all. You see Peter turns out to be the perfect example to push towards being submissive.

18 As Jesus was walking beside the Sea of Galilee, he saw two brothers, Simon called Peter and his brother Andrew. They were casting a net into the lake, for they were fishermen. 19 "Come, follow me," Jesus said, "and I will send you out to fish for people." 20 At once they left their nets and followed him.
Matthew 4:18-20 NIV

While Peter and Andrew were casting their net into the lake, Jesus says to them, "Follow me". In so many words, he strongly suggests to them to be submissive unto Him, be humble, and when you do this, you will not only be made a great fisherman, but, a fisher of men. Jesus told Peter and his brother Andrew, in layman terms, that He will save them. He stated that he will place something special in their hearts. If we, too, listen carefully, we can hear or even witness through other avenues in life the same message as Peter. Anybody can be a great fisherman; it just takes hours of practice. Jesus says He can give us all a special gift and make us all fishers of men. I believe Jesus is saying He wants to save us, so in turn, we will be able to help save others, and then they'll do the same for others! This cycle is meant to go on infinitely. It was at that point that Peter began his submissive process. In this message spoken to a congregation, I suggested we all must submit and be more ready and willing. I stated to this congregation that if your pastor asks different members to assist with worship, it'll be in your best interest to abide, submit, and do so if it is within your due bounds.

When we usher, help in the kitchen, sing in the choir, that is being submissive. When we're walking along sidewalks and we make contact with the homeless and that homeless individual asks you for change, if you have it, you should be generous and give. That is being submissive. Or when we selflessly pray for one another, that too is being submissive. These examples can be applied to being submissive, having trust, and belief. By following

Jesus, this will continuously give you favor in reaching your goal of receiving that "Crown of Glory." Peter says he wants us to be shepherds of God's flock. Begin your process in submission along this route as shepherds.

My second point is to humble yourself. The scripture says:

5 clothe yourselves with humility toward one another, because, God opposes the proud but gives grace to the humble.
1 Peter 5:5 NIV

Equip yourself with the character and attribute of being humble. According to scripture, 'God opposes the proud;' in other words, he opposes the selfish and those who knowingly choose to be ignorant. It's in our best interest to strive for humility because God gives His grace to the humble. Think of it as an act of altruism, the selfless concern for the welfare of others. If you begin having selfless concern for others, you, in turn, will receive a reward. *1 Kings 21:29 Have you seen how Ahab has humbled himself before me?* He has humbled himself before me, I will not bring the disaster in his days, *2 Chronicles 12:12 says, And when he humbled himself the wrath of the LORD turned from him, so as not to make a complete destruction. Moreover, conditions were good in Judah.*

It's quite a simple formula! Humility leads to grace; become humble and receive a reward. Throughout my short career in higher education, I've heard several judicial cases. It never ceases to amaze me on how so many students enter their own hearings with an attitude drenched in a selfishness spirit, a negative personality speaking for itself, or a negative character that can be read like an open book, a book that reads: "It's either my way or the highway". This always throws up a red flag that their "Humblemeter" is on zero, and in almost every situation such as this, they are found responsible for their actions. Occasionally, some students are given leniency. Occasionally, some students enter their hearings with a positive special aura, their explanations are genuinely remorseful, their situation has triggered their "Humblemeter", and with that simple act of humility, they receive grace. Be submissive and clothe yourself with humility toward one another; this is how you receive your Crown of Glory.

My last point is to use self-control be and alert. Scriptures says,

8 ...*your enemy the devil prowls around like a roaring lion looking for someone to devour. 9 Resist him, standing firm in the faith, because you know that your brothers throughout the world is undergoing the same kind of sufferings.*
I Peter 5:8-9 NIV

A great pastor preached to me once and said that "it's not good enough to just know the word of God. The devil himself knows the word". We must be careful of his prowling efforts. In a Sunday school conversation, it was verbalized that we're in a world now where a lot of people believe they're at the top of their piety; we have brothers and sisters in Christ who would brag and boast that they've read the Bible several times over, from front to back. Peter teaches the word of Jesus and in so many words, he tells us that that's not enough. The word says that's not enough because we must apply it. Jesus shows us how to resist and stand firm and how to be self-controlled and alert in the all too familiar scriptures from Matthew 4 where he had been led by the Spirit into the wilderness to be tempted by the devil. The scripture reads: ***2 After fasting forty days and forty nights, he was hungry. 3 The tempter came to him and said, "If you are the Son of God, tell these stones to become bread." 4 Jesus answered, "It is written: 'Man shall not live by bread alone, but on every word that*** *comes from the mouth of God.' " 5 Then the devil took him to the holy city and had him stand on the highest point of the temple. 6 "If you are the Son of God," he said, "throw yourself down. For it is written: "He will command his angels concerning you, and they will lift you up in their hands so that you will not strike your foot against a stone.' " 7 Jesus answered him, "It is also written: 'Do not put the Lord your God to the test.' " 8 Again, the devil took him to a very high mountain and showed him all the kingdoms of the world and their splendor. 9 "All this I will give you," he said, "if you will bow down and worship me." 10 Jesus said to him, "Away from me, Satan! For it is written: 'Worship the Lord your God, and serve him only.' " 11 Then the devil left him, and angels came and attended him.* Jesus showed us poise, strength, an example of truly being self-controlled and alert.

Jesus teaches us and Peter followed Jesus and taught us that this is how you "receive your Crown of Glory", by being submissive, being humble, and being self-controlled and alert. And with that, it reads in the scripture,

10 …God of all grace, who called you to his eternal glory in Christ, after you have suffered a little while, will himself restore you and make you strong, firm and steadfast. 11 To him be the power for ever and ever. Amen.
I Peter 5:10-11 NIV

VIII

MESSAGE FROM ABOVE

1 Now the people complained about their hardships in the hearing of the LORD, and when he heard them his anger was aroused. Then fire from the LORD burned among them and consumed some of the outskirts of the camp. 2 When the people cried out to Moses, he prayed to the LORD and the fire died down. 3 So that place was called Taberah, [a] because fire from the LORD had burned among them.
Numbers 11:1-3 NIV

The Lord puts us in different situations and places in our lives for many reasons, most of the time we never know why. He puts different people in our lives for growth, perhaps to gain experience of what may come. Most of us may think we know why, but His reasoning is far beyond our scope of thought. In this message, I want you to understand the importance of accepting where you currently are in life, and knowing that complaining will prevent you from growing. Complaining stunts our growth; the more you complain, the more you are likely to be unhappy. The more are unhappy, the more likely you are to miss your blessing because you're focused on the unhappiness. I want you to lead in a positive manner. You must lead with positive energy because what our children see will ultimately be instilled in them as a foundation.

Have you ever run into a child that's always frowning and upset? Nine times out of ten it's because that child sees the parent or guardian displaying the same characteristics. Have you ever noticed a youth who always gossips unintentionally? It's because that guardian or parent may indeed be telling everybody's business, and that child is surrounded by it every day. Let me enlighten you on understanding the difference between being grateful and ungrateful, having a vision and no vision, and ultimately knowing your blessing. Some of the people in Moses' camp displayed these characteristics. It was unfortunate because some of them had to learn the hard way. I title this message, "Message from above" because with our spiritual hearing, sight, and individual anointing, we should all take time to witness the messages that the Lord puts in our plain sight.

The scripture says in Numbers 11 verse 1, **Now the people complained about their hardships in the hearing of the LORD, and when he heard them his anger was aroused.** Sometimes we must read between the lines to understand what's going on. **Deuteronomy 29:29 says, The secret things belong to the LORD our God, but the things revealed belong to us and to our children forever, that we may follow all the words of this law".**

This tells us that the more we believe, the more will be revealed. In studying this text, the Lord wants to reveal to us the importance of being grateful. The scripture said, **"The Lord heard them."** Moses didn't hear them; Aaron didn't hear them; but, it was the Lord that heard their vocal complaints about hardship. The Lord heard them, and when He heard them, it sent him off the deep end. In the Old Testament, the Lord didn't hesitate to make examples. And he certainly didn't have the patience for the ungrateful. When He heard them, the scripture says, **"His anger aroused."**

He was highly upset, then fire from the LORD burned among them and consumed some of the outskirts of the camp. He either tried to send a message or just get rid of those who complained and were ungrateful. When that fire came down from the people, they cried out to Moses. That tells us that Moses knew nothing about them complaining. Moses then prayed for them because he had compassion for them. With that compassion, the Lord pulled back. We need to use that as a message sent from above, by applying it to our own lives. A while back, on my way to Walmart, I was listening to Joel Osteen and ironically, he touched on what I was intending on writing in this message in terms of being grateful. He talked about the blessings that come along with being grateful, but also recognizing that if we aren't grateful, it can be taken away. The Lord giveth, and the Lord taketh away.

Think about the individual with the not so nice-looking car. On the outside, it's beaten up; it has missing hubcaps, rust, dents, etc. It is the kind of car that you wouldn't want to be caught riding in when trying to impress others. On the inside, that same individual has taken great care of it by keeping the interior clean, shampooing it. It may have a few rips in the seats here and there, but it's loved. The oil change is always kept current, tune up is always completed as needed, and all engine maintenance is kept up accordingly. It may still break down every now and then, but it runs, and most importantly, the owner of this loved vehicle is grateful. Those who are close to me know I have a very similar story. As a man that stands at the height of 6'4, my first vehicle was a white 4-door Geo-Metro. I can't remember the year of the model, but, it was my baby. I made sure I got the oil change when needed; I drove it to my classes and basketball practice through rain, sleet, and snow. No one could tell me anything about my Geo that would place me in a bad space because I had a vehicle that got me from point A to point B and sometimes point C. I was grateful.

The same analogy can be used for clothes. My mother didn't have much to give raising 4 children (that was when I was in middle and high school, she now has a total of 6 children). We are all too familiar with the have and have nots. I happened to have fallen on the side of those who didn't have much, but only in the worldly eyes of others. I didn't own name brand clothes, I didn't wear Jordans or any other shoes that cost $100 and above. I remember the times where I was bitter and ungrateful. As I got older, I understood that things could be worse. What I did have was clean clothes on my back, clothes that were always starched and pressed. I didn't have holes covered with card board on my feet. I was properly provided for and in the end, grateful.

The more the Lord recognizes how grateful you are, the more you receive blessings. The more ungrateful you are, the more you miss your blessings. Fortunately for me, I began to recognize those blessings. Take care of what God has given you, wait, and watch more be produced from it.

As you have read thus far, there were some people in Moses' camp who were ungrateful. Scriptures says, **4 The rabble with them began to crave other food, and again the Israelites started wailing and said, "If only we had meat to eat! 5 We remember the fish we ate in Egypt at no cost—also the cucumbers, melons, leeks, onions, and garlic. 6 But now we have lost our appetite; we never see anything but this manna!"** If you don't know what Manna is, the scripture says, **7 The manna was like coriander seed and looked like resin. 8 The people went around gathering it, and then ground it in a hand mill or**

crushed it in a mortar. They cooked it in a pot or made it into loaves.

The Israelites said "at no cost." They said they had cucumbers, melons, leaks, onions, and garlic at no cost. But it was a cost; they were slaves, and from the looks of it, they still were slaves, mentally. They were so ungrateful at that time that they forgot their ultimate goal. Their vision began to fade. You see, Moses had purpose and vision, but these selected individuals had none and forgot all that was promised in this new land in which they were traveling to. We too must be careful that our vision within our own personal journey doesn't fade or get cloudy.

My vision nearly faded away due to my own actions. During my high school years, I was mentally lost. Skipping classes, verbally lashing out at those who were present to only help me, and simply not giving a damn. The vision of graduating from high school was just as blurry as an early foggy morning. As I previously stated, I recognized my blessings after I complained about not having what my peers had, all while having more than enough while all my needs were being met. It led me to act out to make up for where I thought I lacked. This also led me to hang with the wrong crowd, which led me to fail classes, which led me to not graduating on time, which led me to come back for a 5th year of high school. That was the Lord's way of teaching me. The blessings that I missed were the classes before me. Here I was exemplifying ungrateful behaviors while some people in other countries don't have the educational opportunity I had. There were times I nearly missed my blessing for lack of vision. But, I eventually listened to my heart and I followed His word. This led me to fulfil and crystalize that blurry goal of graduating. It also led me towards another goal and vision of mine of going to college and playing collegiate basketball.

Just a few years ago, my vision became blurry again as I woke up day after day, week after week, wishing I was back in Florida. I had taken my family to a place where retirees would go after the long years of winters up north. My wife and I made a conscious choice to pick up and come back North for the sake of our children, for the sake of self-improvement, and for the family. Somewhere along this journey, I almost forgot the importance of appreciating the blessings sent from above.

An entire year being back up North, I acted as an unappreciative Israelite living in the past. I often imagined walking on different beaches with daily summer's sunshine, just as the Israelites did as they reminisced and yearned for the cucumbers, melons, and leaks. I was ungrateful, and my vision began to fade. The bigger picture was to not only have our children in a better school system but for me to gain better professional experience in the field I love so dearly. Since then I have done my best to be obedient again, and that renewed vision has come to fruition. My wife has reaped great reward by enrolling and graduating with a master degree in social work from the University of Illinois at Urbana-Champaign. I came back to the realization that if I continue to practice losing sight and vision, it will definitely hinder the blessings that are yet to come.

This scripture was so powerful, it opened my eyes. I wanted to prepare something to motivate and change lives through the Lord and ended up preaching to myself. How divine is that? We now know or are reminded of the importance of being grateful and having a vision; you also must recognize and know your blessings. I often speak about how the devil is the author of confusion. That confusion was in the midst of Moses camp just as it was among Christ as He fasted. It enters our household, our schools, and our place of employment. Confusion is right in our very own churches. What we cannot do is let that confusion develop in us.

Kendrick Lamar is a very popular hip-hop/rap artist. He is said to be this era's new Public Enemy, an offspring of Tupac Shakur. If most of you can remember, Public Enemy had more of a radical approach in empowering the Black community, just as Tupac was a revolutionist for the same cause. Kendrick Lamar seems to be taking more of a spiritual approach in uplifting the Black community. In one of his albums, he talks about this person called Lucy. For weeks, I tried to decipher and figure out what he meant by continuously referring to this Lucy person. Understand this, once my wife and I run into a puzzle, it's hard for us to really get sleep until we figure it out. She came in one day and said she finally figured out who this Lucy person was; in Kendrick's albums, Lucy is short for Lucifer, the adversary, the devil. This person or entity that was being referred to was causing confusion. The character in the album kept giving different alternatives, opposite of what's ordained from the Lord for one to be successful. We must be aware of the Lucys because if we fall short of mingling with the evil Lucy, it will indeed cause us blessings. Don't lose what's already laid out for you. Be grateful, have and keep your vision, recognize your blessings. Adhere to the messages from above.

IX
NEW BEGINNING

18 "Forget the former things; do not dwell on the past. 19 See, I am doing a new thing Now it springs up; do you not perceive it? I am making a way in the wilderness and streams in the wasteland. Isaiah 43:18-19 NIV

Past events, setbacks, purpose, and peace are important. In no particular order, I want you all to think about these 4 points. Every so often, we think about this thing called the past, and we think about how the past is such a hindrance on who we are today. We think that if we could time travel then we'd change what we did or used to do to feel better about who we currently are. Some of us think about the past and begin to develop a chip on our shoulder; some of us even develop a state of paranoia. Some of us experience sorrow, heart ache, and depression. Tell me why some of us rarely look at the past as a blessing in disguise. In this message, I want you to know that what you've gone through in the past has created who you are at this very moment. Past events, setbacks, and purpose were also what David went through before he received peace. As I wrote this text, I read one of T.D. Jakes many books entitled Power meets Potential and it was while operationalizing the text that the Holy Spirit communicated with me. It was revealed to me that understanding the past is to understand our purpose. Understanding our purpose is to mentor at our local community centers and schools, and to work with youth that most have written off.

The past is the very thing that not only helps us understand, but it's used as a tool to lead us toward our purpose. In knowing how the past can better help us, rather than hinder us, we should only look forward to new beginnings.

When we think about new beginnings, it's natural to think about the setbacks; some good and some bad. It's natural to think about what obstacles may be placed in the way of our future goal of creating a new. A friend and I once conversed about how she has this burning desire inside of her to preach the Lord's Word, but according to her denomination, women are not allowed to preach in the pulpit. Together we concluded that she should not lean on man's understanding, but to lean on God and let Him reveal to her if she should preach or not. I simply told her what my very good friend TaMario Howze, once told me. He said, "We need to be focused on kingdom building and sometimes that comes with God transitioning us to a different or higher level." I told her that what she is dealing with is simply a setback, whether good or bad. It's a setback that'll lead her toward her own spiritual outcome. Some of us say on Wednesday how we want to attend a church service or Sunday school, until we wake up late or run into traffic, a setback, whether good or bad. You see, we often need to have these setbacks to slow us down and give us time to figure out where we should be spiritually. It helps us to get our mind stayed on the Lord before we get to the church to properly receive a message. Setbacks are simply used as a mechanism to strategically slow us down.

What if I told you that our own pride can be a setback in life that can lead us to a prosperous outcome? Would you believe me? We truly can be led to a prosperous outcome, but only if we are obedient. As a sophomore playing basketball in college, a team meeting was called. As we all filed into a classroom for the team meeting, I already had a defiant attitude with a built-up wall blinding and blocking my blessings. If anyone knows me well, one thing they can attest to was that I used to wear my feelings on my sleeve, in my facial expressions, and I was very vocal. To some extent, I still am today. My coach, who now also is an AME preacher, asked the team while giving his many motivating speeches, something along the lines of why we didn't act a certain way or complete a certain task. I was the only one that answered, and stated that it was because I had too much pride. He looked at me and said, "Too much pride will kill you!" The following scriptures tell us about the wrong pride one can possess. *2 Chronicles, his pride led to his downfall. Proverbs 11:2, when pride comes, then comes disgrace but with humility comes wisdom.* That very moment was a mental setback for me and is now a past event that I lean on to remind me not to be too proud.

Let's dig into scripture and talk a bit about David's setbacks and how he received peace. David had a great purpose; his purpose was to provide for Israel as a King anointed by the Lord. David had even been delivered from the hands of Saul. This tells us that there was a reason for his existence; he fulfilled this purpose and became one of the best King's within what was called the golden age. As a great king, he too had past events which were also his setbacks. In 2 Samuel 11:2-14, the scripture reads as such:

2 One evening David got up from his bed and walked around on the roof of the palace. From the roof he saw a woman bathing. The woman was very beautiful, 3 and David sent someone to find out about her. The man said, "She is Bathsheba, the daughter of Eliam and the wife of Uriah the Hittite." 4 Then David sent messengers to get her. (Now she was purifying herself from her monthly uncleanness.) She came to him, and he slept with her. Then she came back home. 5 The woman conceived and sent word to David, saying, "I am pregnant." 6 So David sent this word to Joab (A relative

*of David and one of his Chief Warriors): "Send me Uriah the Hittite."
And Joab sent him to David. 7 When Uriah came to him, David
asked him how Joab was, how the soldiers were and how the war was
going. 8 Then David said to Uriah, "Go down to your house and
wash your feet." So Uriah left the palace, and a gift from the king was
sent after him. 9 But Uriah slept at the entrance to the palace with all
his master's servants and did not go down to his house. 10 David was
told, "Uriah did not go home." So he asked Uriah, "Haven't you just
come from a military campaign? Why didn't you go home?" 11 Uriah
said to David, "The ark and Israel and Judah are staying in tents, [a]
and my commander Joab and my lord's men are camped in the open
country. How could I go to my house to eat and drink and make love
to my wife? As surely as you live, I will not do such a thing!" 12 Then
David said to him, "Stay here one more day, and tomorrow I will
send you back." So Uriah remained in Jerusalem that day and the
next. 13 At David's invitation, he ate and drank with him, and David
made him drunk. But in the evening Uriah went out to sleep on his
mat among his master's servants; he did not go home. 14 The next
morning David sent a letter back with Uriah to Joab. The letter read,
"Put Uriah out in front where the fighting is fiercest. Then withdraw
from him so he will be struck down and die."*

Oh, what a setup for such a setback! We don't only have to catch drama like this on VH-1 or BET, all we have to do is open the good book where you can get your reality fix and a lesson all at the same time.

The scripture went on to say that David put Uriah in an area where those who were attacking were the strongest. When men came out to fight the battle, a number of men in David's army were slain; most importantly, Uriah was killed. This news, of course, was sent back to Uriah's wife. Over time, she found solace in David. Thereafter, he took her as his wife and they had a son. This in crafted act angered the Lord. Again, we don't have to only catch drama like this on VH-1 or BET, all we have to do is open the good book where you can get your reality fix and a lesson all at the same time.

1 The Lord sent Nathan to David. When he came to him, he said, "There were two men in a certain town, one rich and the other poor. 2 The rich man had a very large number of sheep and cattle, 3 but the poor man had nothing except one little ewe lamb he had bought. He raised it, and it grew up with him and his children. It shared his food, drank from his cup and even slept in his arms. It was like a daughter to him.
4 "Now a traveler came to the rich man, but the rich man refrained from taking one of his own sheep or cattle to prepare a meal for the traveler who had come to him. Instead, he took the ewe lamb that belonged to the poor man and prepared it for the one who had come to him." 5 David burned with anger against the man and said to Nathan, "As surely as the Lord lives, the man who did this must die! 6 He must pay for that lamb four times over, because he did such a thing and had no pity." 7 Then Nathan said to David, "You are the man!..."
2 Samuel 12:1-7 NIV

The Lord had given David so much; he was given wealth and protection, and he was even given Israel and Judah. He would be rewarded as much as he wanted if he would just ask. His distasteful ways were so bitter and self-centered. These setbacks—of murder and adultery, all for selfish reasons—were displeasing in the eyes of the Lord.

11 This is what the LORD says: 'Out of your own household I am going to bring calamity on you. Before your very eyes I will take your wives and give them to one who is close to you, and he will sleep with your wives in broad daylight. 12 You did it in secret, but I will do this thing in broad daylight before all Israel.
2 Samuel 12:11-12 NIV

After this, David realized his sins against the Lord. Nathan told David that the Lord forgives him, but the results of this will be the death of his son. The child that Uriah's wife had given David was struck by the Lord and he became ill. David fasted and spent nights in sackcloth feelings heartfully sorry for his misdoings. His son died on the seventh day. When David realized the baby boy had died, he cleaned himself up, went into the house of the Lord and worshipped.

What do we usually look for when we come to the house of the Lord? We search for peace. David was a man who stumbled and fell hard; yet, through confession and worship, he was cleansed to walk even closer to the Lord. David's actions consist of selfishness and schemes that led to adultery, murder, loss and sorrow. His storm was his setback before he received peace. Know that in this life, you're either getting ready to go through something, you're already going through it, or you're coming out; we go through several storms, some light and some heavy. Last year, we all had storms, know that this year, presently, will be where the sun peaks through the clouds, shines on you and brings you a brighter day. What ever happened that wasn't pleasing to you, pray about it, pray to the Lord, know that Jesus gave himself for our sins, and repent of it.

Your setbacks will not be your end result. Find your peace, pray for your purpose.

Create a new day for your life, amid all the circumstances that you're facing. Know that everything that you think is binding you and holding you down won't last forever. Stand tall, surround yourselves with winners, and trust in the Lord. At this moment, don't allow past events and setbacks to come in and steal the purpose and peace in your new beginning.

X
SANKOFA

8 Finally, all of you, be like-minded, be sympathetic, love one another, be compassionate and humble. 9 Do not repay evil with evil or insult with insult. On the contrary, repay evil with blessing, because to this you were called so that you may inherit a blessing.
1 Peter 3:8-9

In the past 3-5 years, our country has dealt with a multitude of unjustified fatal incidents. The world saw on a public media stage how a young teenager's life was taken during a fatal dispute while walking home. Another tragic incident, of course, ends with the life of another teenager playing his music too loud and suddenly his life was snatched. The world also witnessed a man breathe his last breath on national television because of his past history and the selling of cigarettes. We then witnessed the unrest of citizens speaking out and protesting due to the outburst of a Ferguson, MO teenager. This may remind many of the unrest and protests from the 1950s and 60s. The theme for this message is surrounded around unity. The scripture above tells us how to act and respond as believers. But, somewhere along the way, as American citizens, as a people, I believe that some of us have forgotten the way and purpose that leads us to unity. In the midst of this country's turmoil, I am here to assist by way of this message and inspiration to help you get that unity back. Allow me to give you a simple formula to ponder upon. This formula is comprised of love and humility. I believe that all of us possess this, but sometimes we tend to forget or lose these two simple ingredients. The title of this last message is

"Sankofa", which simply means, to return and fetch what was once lost.

"You can only become truly accomplished at something you love. Don't make money your goal. Instead, pursue the things you love doing and then do them so well that people can't take their eyes off of you."[1] -Maya Angelou

At this stage in my career, I've worked at a few universities before God led me here to Illinois. While supervising and mentoring the many students that I have, and while working with the many colleagues that I have, it never ceases to amaze me how our end goal has been skewed from graduating and simply to being successful. For us as professionals, we have gone from leading and motivating to focusing on how much money we can make or how much professional and political respect we can gained. I too have also been guilty of this. What happens in our lives that make us change and lose focus of the goals we once set? The goal of simply achieving and enjoying the ride has turned into a secondary or short-term goal. What changes us? Is it simply growth or is it a specific distraction? What actually changes our appetite? I'm not talking about the appetite in which we would go to a fast food restaurant or food court in the local mall; and I'm not talking about fulfilling our hunger with the snacks from a corner store or bodega.

What I am alluding to is the spiritual appetite, that spiritual appetite that communicated with us in some form or fashion and motivated us before we got to where we are today—living and breathing, for some of us, working or attending school. I mean don't get me wrong, making a high

---

[1] "A Quote by Maya Angelou." Quote by Maya Angelou: "You can only become truly accomplished at something", www.goodreads.com/quotes/4749-you-can-only-become-truly-accomplished-at-something-you-love.

five or six figure salary would be great, or as my students would say, it would be "lit"! The high income would be lit, but as Sister Maya Angelou once stated, "Don't make money your goal…pursue the things you love doing and then do them so well that people can't take their eyes off of you." I believe that one can only be truly accomplished at something truly loved. What do you love? I love to mentor; I love to inspire; and I love to guide and motivate. I truly feel that doing this is part of my calling. But, when I became a higher education professional, I knew only part of this because I lost sight of my love and the love for others along the way.

My goal to find those students and help them along their way to success turned into, how soon I can get a doctoral degree to simply say that I have a Ph.D.? To simply say I'm Dr. Robertson instead of simply being "Prince", the man that left a legacy of helping to graduate hundreds upon hundreds of students. I lost sight of what I love to selfishly compete with colleagues at national conferences instead of rubbing shoulders to pick up the best trend-setting practice. Oh, how easily we can be distracted from our ultimate goal and love, and almost all of the time, it's when we fall flat on our faces and experience that setback. It's those seasonal storms by way of sickness or falling out with someone, or receiving an unsatisfying grade or lacking in performance on the job that breaks us down and brings us back to reality. I believe that those setbacks are simply the work of the Lord that reminds us that we can't get too big for our britches, as some of our elders once told us. I urge you all to stay true and love what you do, love one another, and stay focused on your goal. Reach back and fetch that love that may have been was once lost.

1 Corinthians 13:13 says, and now these three remain: faith, hope, and love. But the greatest of these is love.

"There is no better than adversity. Every defeat, every heartbreak, every loss, contains its own seed, its own lesson on how to improve your performance next time."[2]
-El Hajj Malik El Shabazz, better known as Minister Malcolm X

In one of the earlier messages, I mentioned how I talked to a congregation about how to be humble, and how being humble will lead us to receive our crown of glory. I also came from the book of 1 Peter and I wanted to focus on the premise that everyone goes through something challenging at some point in their life. The message I wanted to deliver was that every time you go through a challenging situation, depending on what it is, it should humble you just a bit. Remember how devoted Peter was to Jesus Christ, but, before he became devoted he had to go through his own trials and tribulations. You see Peter was known to be a bit unbecoming and stubborn. He was also known to be a bit too brash in his actions. But he was also known to be one of Jesus first and closest followers and was very passionate about the ultimate mission. Brother Malcolm X, too, like Peter was also known to be a bit unbecoming and too brash in his actions, but he too also had a lot of passion about his mission. Brother Malcolm's passion was of course to be an uplifting figure to the Black race in the days of the civil rights fight.

As some of us may or may not know, in his autobiography written with the help of Alex Haley, he told us, in so many words, how he was a very proud man. He was also very intelligent and knew right from wrong, including understanding his influence on others. I would even go as far as to say that he, at one time, was ignorant of the magnitude of his powerful

---

[2] "Quotes." Malcolm X, 10 Feb. 2015, Malcolm.com/quotes/.

leadership. It was during his pilgrimage to the Holy Mecca that he ran into a man who communicated to him that his practice of Islam in the United States was incorrect. This humbled Brother Malcolm; this was his lesson on how to improve himself. Like Peter and Brother Malcolm, I too had my days of facing opposition, rules, and regulations of authority as I was engaged in drinking, smoking marijuana, being a playboy, etc. Knowing that I had some sort of leadership ability, I was simply naïve to the skillset. But then one day, truth and humility were revealed to me when having met the Lord, and having Him communicate with me letting me know that it was time to change. The results of me not changing is something I would not want to adorn.

I think back to how vulnerable I felt as a college student, wanting to get things done on my own, dealing with anxiety, stress, death, academic struggles, all while having the resources at the tip of my fingers, but I was too proud to ask for help. It took a lot for me to breakdown and move forward, and to learn that I couldn't do it on my own. Scripture tells us **When pride comes in, then comes disgrace, but with humility comes wisdom. -Proverbs 11:2.** See Peter as a life example, take heed to Brother Malcolm too. Both are examples of people who I learned from while reaching back to fetch that humility that was lost.

"I often feel like saying, when I hear the question 'People aren't ready', that it's like telling a person who is trying to swim, 'Don't jump in that water until you learn how to swim.' When actually you will never learn how to swim until you get in the water. And I think people have to have an opportunity to develop themselves and govern themselves."[3] -Reverend Dr. Martin Luther King, Jr.

---

[3] King Jr., Martin Luther. Interview by Etta Moten Barnett. March 6, 1957 https://kinginstitute.stanford.edu/king-papers/documents/interview-etta-moten-barnett. Accessed 15 May. 2016

A lot of us have never met Reverend Dr. Martin Luther King, Jr., but what we do know is the legacy that he left behind of truly showing us his compassion. All of the movies and documentaries are well founded but, if we really attempt to understand his message as to why he did what he did, we have no choice but to notice the true essence of compassion. In fact, if we think back to several of our civil rights leaders, we would notice the characteristic of compassion. Imagine if we utilized compassion on a daily basis. As I stand on the shoulders of my mentors, as many of us also are doing, I can't help to think to myself, "Why does it seem so much harder?" We've heard about the segregated classrooms, buses, restaurants, and bathrooms. It seems as if we've come so far, but yet it seems as if we are still standing in the same place, stagnant to the ways of the world and its issues. My colleagues will tell you that I recite what one of my mentors told me that still resonates even more today. The late, Brother Willie E. Thompson stated, "History always repeats itself". When I first heard him say those words, it dug a deep hole into my soul. I now continue to hear those words repeated in my mind and to reminisce on the leader that he was. I now know he wanted us, as his students, to not just know that history repeats itself, but in the midst of it, we also have to know that we have an innate ability to make a change. As higher education professionals, we always tell our students to become change agents, but how many of us hear this from our mentors and leaders and actually believe it?

As I close out the last message in this book, I want you to know that we stand on the shoulders of those who possessed love and humility, those who fought not just to make things easier for us, but to help us to understand the ways of the world. We have no choice but to succeed, to volunteer in our community, to help others in time of need, to treat each other as brothers and sisters, to pass classes, to graduate, and to be successful! When times get hard, I urge you to not just think about how history repeats itself, but to think about whose succession you will lean on as motivation and how you can positively prevent it from repeating.

SANKOFA my brothers and sisters, return and fetch what was once lost.

NOTES

NOTES

MOTIVATIONS

MOTIVATIONS

PRAYERS

PRAYERS

ABOUT THE AUTHOR

Prince Robertson was born in Harlem, NY and raised in Saginaw, Michigan. He received his Bachelor of Art degree from Saginaw Valley State University. He earned his Master of Science in Education from Southern Illinois University Carbondale and he is now embarking on a doctoral degree in Education from the University of Illinois at Urbana-Champaign. Whether he is on a college campus, in the community, or in the pulpit, he spreads a message of love, encouragement, and faith. By mentoring and serving as a surrogate father to many of his students, he has helped to change the life trajectories of many of the young people who he has served.

Made in the USA
Las Vegas, NV
11 September 2021